*Compiled by the
Daughters of St. Paul*

BOOKS & MEDIA

Boston

With ecclesiastical approval.

All rights reserved. No part of this book may be reproduced or transmitted in any form or by any means, electronic or mechanical, including photocopying, recording or by any information storage and retrieval system, without permission in writing from the publisher.

Copyright © 1981, Daughters of St. Paul

Printed and published in the U.S.A. by Pauline Books & Media, 50 Saint Pauls Avenue, Boston MA 02130-3491.

www.pauline.org

Pauline Books & Media is the publishing house of the Daughters of St. Paul, an international congregation of women religious serving the Church with the communications media.

6 7 8 9 10 11 12   08 07 06 05 04 03

Contents

Introduction 7
Christian Names for Boys 9
Christian Names for Girls 29
Patron Saints 53

PATRON SAINTS

Introduction

From the earliest times, the Church has encouraged parents to give their children baptismal names which bear some Christian significance. And so, the names of martyrs, of holy men and women—"greats" in the living of the Christian vocation—have become a favorite source of names.

"The name given the child at Baptism," writes the late Cardinal Cushing, "should be a saint's name. Why a saint's name at Baptism? The saint chosen acts in the role of a sponsor for the child in the courts of heaven. We believe that our Guardian Angel, assigned to us by God at our birth, protects and guides us throughout life. Likewise, our patron saint follows our earthly career with more than kindly interest. Do you know the life story of your patron saint? Do you pray often to that saint for help and guidance? You should, because he or she is your firm friend before the throne of God."

By taking a Christian name, we not only honor "the saints who have suffered and been glorified with Christ" (Lit. 104), but we also "seek from the saints example in their way of life, fellowship in their communion, and aid by their intercession" (Ch. 5). A true spiritual patrimony is given the child; "his saint" is not just a name, but also a pledge of a lifelong patron, a special intercessor or friend in heaven.

This pamphlet includes all types of names to suit all sorts of tastes. All are Christian names, and the feast days following each entry are either those listed in the current Church calendar or those assigned by custom or popular usage (for saints not appearing in the present calendar). This makes possible the celebration of one's "name day," a practice very helpful for introducing younger family members to their patron, and deepening their love and knowledge of them.

A second section gives handy and interesting information on the saints as patrons or protectors for those in particular professions or occupations, as well as others to be invoked in times of special need.

Christian Names for Boys

A

Aaron, July 3
Abban, Oct. 27
Abel, Dec. 2
Abraham, Oct. 9
   Abram
Absolan, March 2
Achillius the
   Great, May 12
Achim (Joachim),
   Aug. 16
Achmed, Dec. 24
Adalbert, April 23
   Adelbert
Adam, Dec. 24
Adelard, Jan. 2
Adolph, June 17
   Adolfo, Adolphe,
   Adolphus, Dolph
Adrian, Sept. 8
   Hadrian
Adrien, April 1
Aeneas (Angus),
   March 11
Aidan, Aug. 31
Alan, Oct. 26
   Alain
Alaric, Sept. 29
Alban, June 22
   Albany, Albin

Alberic, Jan. 26
Albert, Nov. 15
   Albrecht, Alberto,
   Albertino, Elbert
Albian, June 10
Albin, March 1
Alcuin, May 19
Aldric, Jan. 7
Alexander, Feb. 26
   Alessandro, Alesan-
   dre, Alistair
Alexis, July 17
   Alexian, Alexio,
   Alexios, Aleixo,
   Alexe, Alessio, Alexius
Alfred, Aug. 15.
Allan, Jan. 12
   Allen
Alleyn, Feb. 22
Aloysius, June 21
   Alois, Aloisio, Aloys
Alphonse, Aug. 1
   Alfons, Alfonso,
   Alonso, Alphonso
Altman, Aug. 8
Alton (Alto), Feb. 9
Alvin, Oct. 1
Amadeus, Jan. 28
   Amyot

Amand, Feb. 6
Ambrose, Dec. 7
   Ambrosio, Ambroise, Ambrozi, Bruce
Americus (Emmeric), Nov. 4
   Almeric, Americo, Amerigo, Amery, Amory
Amos, March 31
Anastasius, Dec. 19
Anatole, July 3
   Anatol
Ancel (Lancelot), June 27
Andrew, Nov. 30
   Anders, Andre, Andrea, Andrus, Andres, Anderson
Angelo, May 5
Angus, March 11
Anselm, April 21
   Ansel, Anselme, Anselmo
Ansgar, Feb. 3
Anthony (abbot, Jan. 17; Claret, Oct. 24; of Padua, June 13; Zaccaria, July 5)
   Anton, Antoni, Antonie, Antonio
Antonine, May 10

Aquinas (Thomas), Jan. 28—Aquin
Archibald, March 27
Ardan, Feb. 11
Aristo, Dec. 3
Armand, Jan. 23
Armon, July 31
Arnold, March 14
   Arnald, Arnaud, Arne, Arno, Arnoldo, Arend, Arnoul
Arsene, July 19
Artemus, Jan. 24
Arthur, Dec. 11
   Arturo, Artur
Ashley (Bl. Ralph), March 7
Athanasius, May 2
Aubert, Sept. 10
Aubin, March 1
   Aubert
Aubrey, Nov. 14
Augustine, Aug. 28 (of Canterbury) May 27
   Auguste, Augustin, Augustino, Austin, Austen, Gus

B

Baptist (St. John the), June 24
   Baptiste

Bardo, June 10
Barlow, Sept. 10
  (Bl. Ambrose)
Barnabas, June 11
  Barnaby
Barnard, Jan. 23
Barr (Finbar), Sept. 25
Barrion, Sept 25
  Barry
Bartholomew, Aug. 24
  Bartek, Bartel,
  Barthole, Bathleme,
  Bartlett, Bartley,
  Barton, Bertel,
  Bartolomeo
Basil, Jan. 2
  Basile, Basine, Vasili
Bastien (Sebastian),
    Jan. 20
Becket (St. Thomas),
    Dec. 29
Bede, May 25
Beltram, March 1
Benedict, July 11
  Benedic, Bendik,
  Benedik, Benedicto,
  Benito, Bennett,
  Benedetto
Benjamin, March 21
Berchmans (St. John),
    Aug. 13
Bernard, Aug. 20

Barend, Barnaro,
Bernardino, Barnett,
Bernardo, Bernhard,
Berns, Burnet

Bernardine, May 20
Bernward, Nov. 20
Berthold, March 29
Bertin, Sept. 5
Bertran, Jan. 24
Bertrand, June 6
  Bertram, Berton,

Beverly (John B.), May 7
Blaine, Aug. 11
Blaise (Blase), Feb. 3
  Blaze
Blane, Aug. 10
  Blaine
Bonaventure, July 15
Boniface, June 5
  Bonifaze
Boris, July 24
Borromeo (St. Charles),
    Nov. 4
Boswell (Boisil), July 7
Brandan, Oct. 20
Brannock, Jan. 7
Brendan, May 16
Brennan, May 6
Brian, March 22
  Brien, Bryan
Briant (Bl. Alex), Dec. 1

Brinstan, Nov. 4
  Bristan
Brogan, Sept. 17
Bruce (Ambrose), Dec. 7
Bruno, Oct. 6
Bryce, Nov. 13
Burton (Bertinus), Sept. 5
Byron (Birinus), Dec. 3

C

Caesar, Aug. 27
  Cesar
Caius, April 22
Cajetan, Aug. 7
Caleb, Oct. 27
Callen, Nov. 28
Callistus, Oct. 14
  Calixtus
Camillus, July 14
  Camille, Comillo
Campion (Edmund), Dec. 1
Canisius, Dec. 21
Cary, Jan. 3
Casimir, March 4
  Casmir, Kasmir
Casper, Jan. 28
  Caspar
Cass, Aug. 13
Cecil, Feb. 1
Celestine, May 19

Charles (Borromeo, Nov. 4; Lwanga, June 3)
  Cahil, Carel, Carol, Carl, Carlo, Carlos, Carroll, Charlet, Charlot, Karl, Karel, Karol, Carlton
Chester (Ceslaus), July 17
Christopher, July 25
  Christophe, Christof
Chrysostom, Jan. 27
Ciro (Cyriac), Aug. 8
Clair (Clarus), Nov. 4
Clarence, April 25
Claret (St. Anthony), Oct. 24
Claude, June 6
  Claudio
Claus (Nicholas), Dec. 6
Clement, Nov. 23
  Clem, Clemence, Clemento, Clemente
Clovis (Louis), Aug. 25
Coleman (Bl. Edward), Dec. 1
Colin (Nicholas), Dec. 6
Colman, Nov. 24
Columba, June 9
Columban, Nov. 23
Conald, Sept. 24
Conan, March 8

Conon, Feb. 26
Conrad, Feb. 19
   Court
Constantine, July 27
   Kurt, Curt
Cornelius, Sept. 16
   Corney, Neal, Nelson, Corneille
Cosmas, Sept. 26
Credan, Aug. 19
Crescent (Cresentius), April 19
Cronan, April 28
Cullan, May 21
Cuthbert, March 20
Cyprian, Sept. 16
   Cyprien
Cyrano, June 16
   Cyran, Cyrin
Cyril, Feb. 14 (Alexandria), June 27
   Cyrill, Cyrille, Cirilo (Cyril of Jerusalem), March 18
Cyrus, Jan. 31

D

Damarius, Sept. 30
Damasus (St. John, Dec. 4; Damasus I, Dec. 11)
Damian, Sept. 26
   Damien, Damio
Daniel, July 21
   Danil, Dannel, Danny
Darius, Dec. 19
David, Dec. 29
   Dawid
Dennis, Oct. 9
   Denez, Denis, Dennet, Denys, Dinis
Deodatus, April 24
Dermit, March 2
Desire (Desiderius), Sept. 16
Devereaux, Nov. 14
   Devereau
Dewey (David), March 1
Diago (James), July 25
   Diego
Dietrich (Theobald), June 30
Dimitri (Demetrius) Oct. 8
   Dimitar
Dion, July 6
Dionysius, Oct. 9
Dismas, March 25
Dominic, Aug. 8
   Diminick, Domingo, Domenico
Donald, July 15
   Don, Donnie
Donan, April 17
Donard, March 24
Donat, March 24

Donatus, Aug. 7
Duane, Feb. 11
Dunstan, May 19
Durban (Urban), May 25
  Durbin
Durdan, Sept. 5
Dustan, July 11

E

Eamon (Edmund), Nov. 16
Earl (Herluin), Aug. 26
Eberhard, June 22
Edbert, May 6
Edfrid, Oct. 26
Edgar, July 8
Edmund, Nov. 16
  Edmond, Tedmund
Edwald, March 23
Edward, Oct. 13
  Edsel, Edson, Eduard
  Edvard, Ward
Edwin, Oct. 12
Egbert, April 24
Eldred, March 13
Elgar, June 14
Elias, July 20
  Ellis, Eliot, Elliott,
  Eli, Elson
Eligius, Dec. 1

Elmer, Aug. 28
Elvis, Feb. 22
Elwin, Feb. 22
Emery, Nov. 4
Emetrius, March 3
  Emmett
Emil, Feb. 1
  Emile
Emilian, Feb. 8
Emmanuel, July 10
  Emanuel, Emminuel
Emmeric, Nov. 4
  Americo, Americus,
  Amery, Emery,
  Emory
Enoch, March 26
Enos, May 1
Enrico (Henry), July 15
Ephrem, June 9
Erasmus, June 2
Eric, May 18
  Erich, Erick, Erik
Ermin, April 25
Ernest, Nov. 7
  Ernesto, Ernst,
  Erneste
Ervan (Ervin), May 29
Esdras, July 13
Esteban (Stephan), Dec. 26
  Etienne
Ethelbert, Feb. 24
Ethian (Ethern), May 27

Eugene, June 2
  Eugen, Eugenio, Gene
Eusebius, Aug. 2
Eustace, Sept. 20
  Eustis
Evan, Aug. 18
Ewald, Oct. 3
Eymard, Aug. 3
Ezechiel, April 10
Ezra, July 13

F

Fabian, Jan. 20
  Fabien
Falco, Feb. 20
Farrel (Fergus), Nov. 18
Faustin, Feb. 15
Felician, June 9
Felipe (Phillip), May 1
Felix, May 18—Felice
Felton (Bl. John), Aug. 8
Ferdinand, May 30
  Fernando, Ferrante, Ferd, Ferde
Fergus, March 29
Fiacre, Aug. 30
Fidelis, Oct. 28; (of Sigmaringen), April 24
Filbert (Philbert), Aug. 20
Finbar, Sept. 25
Finian, Oct. 21
Flavian, Feb. 18
Flobert, Dec. 31
Florens, Dec. 29
Florian, May 4
Floyd (Florentius), June 9
Fortis, May 9
Foster (Vedast), Feb. 6
Francis (of Assisi, Oct. 4; de Sales, Jan. 24; of Paola, April 2; Xavier, Dec. 3)
  Fanchon, Franc, Francisco, Franco, Francois, Franek, Franz, Franklin
Frederick, July 18
  Frederic, Frederico, Fritz
Freeman (Bl. William), Aug. 13
Fridolin, March 6
Fritz, Jan. 16
Fulbert, Oct. 11

G

Gabriel, Sept. 29; (of the Sorrowful Mother), Feb. 27
  Gabrielo, Gavril
Galen, June 22

Gall, Oct. 16
Gallan, Dec. 7
Garcia, Feb. 5
Gardiner (Bl. George), March 7
Garibaldi, Jan. 8
Garnier, July 19
Garret (Gerald), Oct. 13
  Garrett
Gaspar, Dec. 28
Gaston, Feb. 6
Gatian, Dec. 18
Gaudens, Jan. 22
Gedeon, Sept. 1
  Gideon
Genesius, Aug. 25
Gentian, Dec. 11
Geoffrey (Godfrey), Nov. 8
George, April 23
  Georg, Georgt, Giorgio, Gorg, Joris, Jurgen
Gerald, Oct. 13
  Garcia, Girald, Garry, Garret, Garrett, Jarett
Gerard, Oct. 16
  Geraud, Gerhard, Giraud
Gerold, April 19
Geronimo (Jerome), Sept. 30
Gervase, June 19
Gilbert, Feb. 4
  Gilberto, Gisbert, Gibbon
Gildas, Jan. 29
Giles, Sept. 1
  Gilles, Gillet
Giotto (Godfrey), Nov. 8
Giovanni (John), Dec. 27
Girard, Dec. 29
Giuseppe (Joseph), March 19
Goddard, May 4
  Godard
Godfrey, Nov. 8
  Geoffrey, Jeffrey, Joffre
Godwin, Oct. 28
  Goodwin
Gonzaga (St. Aloysius), June 21
Gordian, Sept. 17
  Gordien
Gordius, Jan. 3
  Gordon
Gorman, Aug. 28
Gottfried (Godfrey), Nov. 28
Gottschalk, June 7
Gratian, Dec. 18
Gregory (the Great, Sept. 3; VII, Pope, May 25; Nazianzen, Jan. 2)

Gregor, Gregus,
Gregorio, Gregoire,
Gregg
Griffith, July 1
Guarian, July 27
Guido, Sept. 12
Gunther, Sept. 9
Gustave (Augustus),
Oct. 7
Guy, Sept. 12
   Guidon, Guyon

H

Habert, Dec. 19
Hadrian (Adrian),
Sept. 8
Harding (Stephen),
April 17
Harold, March 25
Hart (Bl. William),
March 13
Harvey, Feb. 17
Harward, Sept. 16
   Harwarld
Henry, July 13
   Hawkins, Henning,
   Hendrik, Henriot,
   Henryk, Heinrich,
   Enrico, Enzio
Herbert, March 20
Herman, April 7
Hermangild, April 13
Hermes, Jan. 4
Hilary, Jan. 13
   Alair, Hilaire, Hilario
Hildebrand, May 25
Hippolytus, Aug. 13
Hobart (Hubert), Nov. 3
Howard (Bl. William),
Dec. 29
Howell (Hywell), Jan. 6
Hubert, Nov. 3
   Hubbard
Hudson (Bl. James),
Nov. 28
Hugh, April 29
   Hugo, Hughes
Humbert, March 4
Humphrey, March 8
   Humphry
Hutchin (Hugh),
April 29
Hyacinth, Aug. 16
   Hyacinthe

I

Iago (James), July 25
Ian (John), Dec. 27
Ignatius (of Loyola,
July 31; of Antioch, Oct. 17)
   Ignace, Ignacy,
   Ignazio
Ildephonsus, Jan. 23

Immanuel, July 10
Innocent, July 28
Irenaeus, June 28
Irvin (Urban), May 25
   Irving
Isaac, Oct. 19
Isaias, July 5
Isidore (Bishop and
   Doctor, April 4;
   farmer, May 15)
   Isidro
Israel, Dec. 22
Ivan, June 24
Ives, April 24
Ivo, May 19
   Ivar

J

Jacinte (Hyacinth),
   Aug. 16
Jacob, Dec. 19
James (the Greater,
   July 25; the Less,
   May 3)
   Jacques, Jacob,
   Jaime, Jamek,
   Jamnik, Jayme,
   Shamus
Januarius, Sept. 19
Jared, March 1
Jareth, Oct. 27

Jarett (Gerald), Oct. 13
Jarmin, Feb. 23
Jarvis, June 19
Jason, July 12
Jasper (Caspar), Dec. 28
Jeffrey (Godfrey), Nov. 8
Jeremias, May 1
   Jeremy
Jerome (Priest and Doc-
   tor), Sept. 30;
   (Emiliani), Feb. 8
   Jeronimo, Geronimo
Jesse, Dec. 29
Jesus *(The name of our
   blessed Lord and Sav-
   ior. Many peoples, out
   of reverence, do not
   use it as a given name;
   others, notably the
   Spanish, taking a dif-
   ferent view, frequent-
   ly give it in Baptism.)*
Joachim, July 26
   Joaquin
Job, May 10
Jocelyn, March 17
   Josselin
Joel, July 13
Jogues (Isaac), Oct. 19
John (Apostle, Dec. 27;
   I, Pope, May 18;
   Baptist de la Salle,
   April 7; Bosco,

Jan. 31; Chrysostom, Sept. 13; Damascene, Dec. 4; de Brebeuf, Oct. 19; Eudes, Aug. 19; Fisher, June 22; Kanty, Dec. 23; Leonardi, Oct. 9; Neumann, Jan. 5; of Capistrano, Oct. 23; of God, March 8; of the Cross, Dec. 14; the Baptist, June 24 [birth], Aug. 29 [beheading]; Vianney, Oct. 4)
Hansel, Ian, Jan, Johan, Johann, Juan, Shawn, Sean, Giovanni, Janek
Jonas, Sept. 21
Jordan, Feb. 15
Joris (George), April 23
Josaphat, Nov. 12
Joseph, (the Worker, May 1; Solemnity, March 19; Calasanz, Aug. 25)
Jose, Josef, Jozef, Giuseppe
Josue, Sept. 1
Jovian, June 1
Joyce, Dec. 13
Jude, Oct. 28
Julian, March 8
Julien
Julius, April 12
Jules
Junius, May 17
Justin, June 1
Justus, Nov. 10

K

Karl (Charles), Nov. 4
Karol, Karel
Kasimir (Casimir), March 4
Kaspar (Caspar), Dec. 28
Kasper, Kass
Kelan (Callen), Nov. 28
Kellen, March 26
Kellog, April 1
Kemble (Bl. John), Aug. 22
Kenelm, July 17
Kennan, Feb. 25
Kenan
Kenneth, Oct. 11
Kenzie

Kent (Kentigern), Jan. 14
Kernan, Nov. 5
Kevin (Keevin), June 3
Kieran, Sept. 9
Kilian, July 8
Killian, Nov. 13
Kim (Korean Martyrs)
Klas (Nicholas), Dec. 6
   Klaas, Klaus
Knute, Jan. 7
Konrad, Feb. 19
Kristopher, July 25
Kurt (Constantine), July 27

L

Ladislaus, June 27
   Ladislas, Lancelot
Lambert, Sept. 17
   Lamberto, Lambrecht
Lancelot, June 27
Landert, Sept. 17
Landry, April 17
Lanfranc, June 23
Laurus, Sept. 30
Lawrence, July 21
   Larkin, Lars, Larse, Lauren, Lauritz, Loren, Lorenz, Lorenzo, Lorin

Lazarus, Dec. 17
   Lazar, Lazare, Lazaro
Leander, Feb. 27
Leo, Nov. 10
   Leon, Lionel, Lee
Leonard, Nov. 26
   Leonardo, Lenny
Leopold, Nov. 15
Lester (Sylvester), Dec. 31
Libertus, Dec. 20
Liguori (St. Alphonsus), Aug. 2
Linus, Sept. 25
Llewelyn, April 7
   Llywelen
Lloyd (Bl. John), July 22
Lockwood (Bl. John), April 13
Loran, Aug. 30
Lothaire, June 14
Lothar, June 14
Louis, Aug. 25
   Clovis, Lewis, Ludwig, Loiz, Luigi, Luis
Loyola (St. Ignatius), July 31
   Lyle
Lucas, June 27
Lucian, Jan. 7
   Lucien
Lucius, March 4

Ludger, March 26
Ludwig, Aug. 25
Luke, Oct. 18
   Lucas, Lukas

M

Macson (Maximus),
   Aug. 13
Magnus, Nov. 5
Mainard, Jan. 21
Major (Maggiorino),
   May 10
Malachy, Nov. 3
   Loughlan
Malcolm, June 3
Manasses, Nov. 5
Manfred, Jan. 28
Manuel, July 10
Marcel, Jan. 16
Marcellinus, June 2
Marcian, June 14
   Marcien
Marcus, Oct. 4
Marian, April 30
Marinus, March 3
Maris, April 26
Marius, Jan. 27
Mark, April 25
   Marc, Marco, Mario
Marnack, March 1
Marne, Sept. 2
Marshall, June 30

Marten, Aug. 18
Martial, June 30
Martin (I, Pope,
   April 13; de Porres,
   Nov. 3; of Tours,
   Nov. 11)
   Martino, Marten,
   Martil, Mertin,
   Marvin
Matthew, Sept. 21
   Mathew, Mathies,
   Mathieu
Matthias, May 14
   Mathias
Maurice, Jan. 15
   Mauras, Mauritz,
   Maury, Moris, Moritz,
   Morris, Murray
Maurilius, Sept. 13
Maximain, June 9
Maximilian, Oct 12
Maximus, Jan. 15
Maynard, May 9
Medard, June 8
Meinrad, Jan. 21
Mel, Feb. 6
Melchior, Jan. 6
Meldan, Feb. 7
Melvin, July 17
Merald, Feb. 23
Merchard, Aug. 24
Meredith (Murtaugh),
   Aug. 13

Methodius, Feb. 14
Michael, Sept. 29
  Micha, Michal,
  Michaud, Michel,
  Michele, Mickel,
  Miguel, Mikel,
  Misha, Mitchell
Miki (St. Paul), Feb. 6
Miles, April 30
  Myles
Milo, Feb. 23
Miron, Aug. 8
Monford, July 2
Moran, Oct. 22
Morand, June 3
More (St. Thomas), July 9
Morgan, May 15
Mortimer, Aug. 12
Moses, Sept. 4
Murdoch, Sept. 2
Myron, Aug. 8

N

Nacaro, Jan 8
Naldo (Ronald), Aug. 20
Napoleon, Aug. 15
Narcissus, March 18
Nathan, Dec. 29
Nathaniel, Aug. 24
Nazaire, July 28
Neal (Cornelius), Sept. 16
  Neil, Nelson
Nepomucene (St. John), May 16
Nereus, May 12
Nestor, Feb. 26
Neville (Alban), June 22
  Nevin
Nicholas, Dec. 6
  Claus, Colin, Klaas,
  Klas, Klaus, Niel, Nico
Nicodemus, Aug. 3
Niles (Nicholas), Dec. 6
Noah, May 2
  Noe
Noel, Dec. 25
Norbert, June 6

O

Obert, Dec. 11
Octavius, Nov. 20
Odemar, May 7
Odilo, Jan. 1
Odilòn, Oct. 28
Odo, Nov. 18
Odoric, Feb. 3
Olaf, July 30
Olier (Oliver), July 11
  Olivier
Omer, Sept. 9

Onesimus, Feb. 16
Onophrius, June 22
Oran, Oct. 27
  Odran
Orestes, Dec. 13
Orlando, May 20
  Orland
Ormond, Jan. 23
Orson, April 13
Osmund, Dec. 4
  Osmond
Oscar, Feb. 3
  Oskar
Oswald, Aug. 5
Otto, July 2
  Eudus, Othello
Owen, March 3

P

Pancras, May 12
Pancratius, March 12
Pantaleon, July 27
Paris, Aug. 5
Paschal, May 17
  Pascal, Pascoe,
  Pasquale, Pasinek
Patrician, Oct. 10
Patrick, March 17
  Paton, Patrig,
  Patrizio, Payton,
  Peyton
Paul (Apostle: Conversion, Jan. 25; Peter and Paul, June 29; Dedication of churches..., Nov. 18; Miki and companions, Feb. 6; of the Cross, Oct. 19)
  Pablo, Paley, Paolo,
  Paulot, Paulus, Pavel,
  Pawel
Paulinus of Nola,
  June 22
Payne (Bl. John), April 2
Pepin, Feb. 21
Percy, Nov. 14
  Percival
Peregrine, May 1
Peter (Apostle: Chair of, Feb. 22; Peter and Paul, June 29; Dedication of churches..., Nov. 18; Canisius, Dec. 21; Chanel, April 28; Chrysologus, July 30; Claver, Sept. 9; Damien, Feb. 21)
  Pearce, Peder, Pedro,
  Peirce, Pierce, Peire,
  Pierot, Perrin, Perry,
  Pierson
Philibert, Aug. 20

Philip (Apostle, May 3;
    Neri, May 26)
    Filipe, Fillipo
Philo, April 25
Phineas, Aug. 12
Pierson (Bl. Walter),
    May 4
Piran, March 5
Pius (V, April 30; X,
    Aug. 21)
Placid, Oct. 5
Plato, April 4
Polycarp, Feb. 23
Pompey, Dec. 14
Pontian, Aug. 13
Porres (Martin), Nov. 3
Princeps, Aug. 22
Prosper, July 25

Q

Quartan, Sept. 3
Quentin, Oct. 31
Quintian, Nov. 13
Quirin, June 4

R

Rainald, Aug. 18
Rainer, Dec. 30
    Rainier
Ralph, July 7
    Randal, Randall,
    Randolph, Randolf,
    Raoul, Rolf, Rollo,
    Roul, Rodolfo
Rambert, June 13
Raphael, Sept. 29
Raymond, Jan. 7
    Raimundo, Ramon
Raynald, Aug. 18
Rayner, Feb. 22
    Raynier
Reginald, April 9
    Reynold, Reinald,
    Reynaud, Reynalt
Regius, June 18
Regnier, Feb. 22
Reinhard, March 7
Reinhold (Reginald),
    Sept. 17
Reinold, Jan. 7
Rembert, Feb. 4
Rene, Feb. 22
    Renier, Reno
Rex, April 9
Rich (Bl. Edmund),
    Nov. 16
Richard, April 3
    Ricardo, Rykart
Robert, Sept. 17
    Robard, Roberto,
    Robin, Hodge
Roch, Aug. 16
    Rock, Roque

Rochester (Bl. John),
   May 4
Roderic, May 13
   Roderick, Roderigo,
   Royce, Ruy
Rodion, April 8
Rodolf, July 27
Roger, Aug. 16
   Rogerio, Rogero,
   Rodger, Rutger, Rory
Roland, Nov. 15
   Rolando, Rowland
Romain, Feb. 28
   Roman
Romano, July 24
Romeo, March 4
Romuald, June 19
Ronald, Aug. 20
Ronan, June 1
Rothard, Oct. 14
Roy (Rufus), Nov. 21
Ruben, Aug. 4
Rubert, May 15
Rudolph, July 27
   Rudolf, Rudolphe,
   Rolf, Rolph, Rollin,
   Rollo
Rufus, Nov. 21
Rupert, March 27
   Ruprecht
Rutger (Roger), Aug. 16
Ruy (Roderic), March 13

S

Sacha (Alexander),
   Feb. 26
   Sanders, Sandor,
   Sandro
Salvator, March 18
Sampson, July 28
   Samson
Samuel, Aug. 20
   Samuele
Sancho (Sanctus),
   June 2
   Sanctos
Sandor (Alexander),
   Feb. 26
   Sandro
Santiago (St. James),
   July 25
Saul, Feb. 16
Savio (Dominic), March 9
Sebastian, Jan. 20
Seran, March 6
Sergius, Sept. 8
   Serge, Sergio
Seth, March 1
Severin, Oct. 23
Severo, Feb. 1
Seward (Siviard),
   March 1
Shamus (James), July 25
Shawn (John), Dec. 27

Sherwood (Bl. Thomas), March 7
Sidney, Sept. 19
Sigefried, Feb. 15
   Sigefrid
Sigfrid, Feb. 15
   Siward
Sigismund, May 1
   Sigmund
Silas, July 13
Silvester, Dec. 31
Silvio, May 31
   Sylvio
Simeon, Feb. 18
Simon, Oct. 28
   Simone
Sinclair (St. Clair), Nov. 4
Sirmion, April 9
Sixtus, Aug. 7
Slade (Bl. Thomas), Oct. 30
Solomon, March 13
Stanislaus, April 11
   Stanislao, Stanko, Stanley
Stephen (first martyr, Dec. 26; of Hungary, Aug. 16)
   Stephan, Stefano
   Stepka, Steven, Esteban
Sulpice, Jan. 17
Sydney, Dec. 10
Sylvester, Dec. 31
Syrus (Syro), June 29

T

Tarsicius, Aug. 15
Tedmund (Edmund), Nov. 16
Tegan, Sept. 9
Terrence, Aug. 29
   Terence
Thaddeus, Oct. 28
Theodore, Nov. 9
   Theodor, Fedor
Theodoric, July 1
   Theodric, Thierry
Thibaud, June 30
Thomas (Apostle, July 3; Aquinas, Jan. 28; Becket, Dec. 29; More, June 22)
   Tomas, Tomasso, Tomaz
Thurstan, March 31
Tiernan, April 4
Tilbert, Sept 7
Timothy, Jan. 26
Titian, Jan. 16

Titus, Jan. 26
   Tito
Tobias, Nov. 2
Toussaint (All Saints),
   Nov. 1
   Toussant
Trajan, Dec. 23
Turibius, March 23
Tybalt, June 30

U

Ubald, May 16
Ugo (Hugh), April 29
Ulmer, July 20
Ulric, July 4
Urban, May 25
Ursino, Nov. 9
Ursus, April 13

V

Valentine, Feb. 14
Valerian, Nov. 27
Valery, April 1
Valter (Walter), June 4
Vardan, Aug. 7
Vernon (Berno), Jan. 13
Vianney (St. John),
   Aug. 4
Viator, Oct. 21
Victor, July 28
Vinard, Oct. 11
Vincent (Deacon,
   Jan. 22; de Paul,
   Sept. 27; Ferrer,
   April 5)
   Vicente, Vincens,
   Vincenti, Vance
Virgil, Nov. 27
Vitalis, Nov. 4
Vitus, June 15
Viviano, Aug. 28
   Vivien
Vladimar, July 15

W

Walter, June 4
   Walther, Walthier,
   Water, Wolter
Ward (Bl. William),
   July 26
Warren, Feb. 6
Webster (Bl. Augustine),
   Feb. 6
Wenceslaus, Sept. 28
   Wenzel, Wenceslas,
   Wesley
Wendelyn, Oct. 21
   Wendel, Wendell
Werner, April 19
Whiting (Bl. Richard),
   Nov. 14
Wilbert, Sept. 11
   Wilbur

Wilfred, April 24
   Wilfrid
Willard, Jan. 10
William, June 25
   Wilhelm, Guillaume,
   Wilson, Quillen,
   Willin, Willis
Willibrod, Nov. 7
Wilmer, July 20
Winfred, Nov. 3
   Winfrid
Wolfgang, Feb. 1
   Wolf
Wright (Bl. Peter), May 19

X

Xavier (St. Francis), Dec. 3
   Xaver, Xavery, Savero
Ximen (Simon), Oct. 28

Y

Yago (James), July 25
   Iago
Yves, May 19
   Yvo

Z

Zachary, Nov. 5
   Zacharius

Christian Names for Girls

A

Ada, Dec. 4
  Adna, Adonetta
Adela, Feb. 24
  Adel, Adella, Adele,
  Adeliza, Della
Adelaide, Dec. 16
  Addie, Adelais,
  Adelecia, Adleta
Adelina, Oct. 20
  Adelia, Adeline
Adilia, Dec. 13
Adolphina, June 17
  Adolphine
Adria, Dec. 2
  Adrianne, Adrienne
Adriana, Aug. 10
Aemilia (Emilian),
  Sept. 11
  Aemiliana
Aerenia, March 8
Agapa, Aug. 8
Agape, Feb. 15
Agatha, Feb. 5
  Agata, Agathe, Aggie
Agnes, Jan. 21
  Agna, Agne, Agneda,
  Agnella, Agnessa,
  Agnese, Agneta, Inez,
  Ines, Inista, Neysa
Aileen (Helen), Aug. 18
Aimee, June 10
  Aime, Amy
Alacoque (St. Margaret
  Mary), Oct. 16
Alane, Nov. 25
  Alanna
Alba, Jan. 17
Alberta, Nov. 15
  Albertina, Albertine,
  Albrette
Albina, Dec. 16
Alda, April 26
  Aldea, Aldine
Alena, June 24
Alexandra, May 18
  Alesandra, Alex-
  andrina, Alexandrine,
  Alexa, Alexine
Alexia, June 29
  Alexis
Alfonsa, Aug. 1
  Alphonsina, Alonsa
Alfreda, Aug. 2
Alfrida, Dec. 8
Alice (Adelaide), Dec. 16
  Alicia, Aline, Alexie,

Alethea, Alisa, Allis,
Alyce, Aleetta,
Alyssa, Ilsa, Allison
Alma (*a title of the
Blessed Mother*)
Alodia, Oct. 22
Aloysia, Sept. 12
Aloys, Aloisia, Aloyza
Alverna, Sept. 14
Alvernia, Laverne
Alvina, June 2
Alvira, March 6
Amabilis, Nov. 1
Amabel, Amabella
Amanda, June 18
Amarna, July 8
Amata, June 10
Ambrosine (Ambrose),
Dec. 7
Amelia, June 2
Amelie
Amy (Amata), June 10
Amicia
Anastasia, Dec. 25
Anatolia, July 9
Anatola
Andrea (Andrew),
Nov. 30
Andrene, Andrina
Androna, Nov. 3
Angela, Jan. 27
Ancela, Angele,
Angelique, Angelita,
Anjela, Aniela
Angelina, July 21
Ann (and Joachim
July 26; Elizabeth
Ann Seton, Jan. 4)
Anna, Anita, Anitra,
Annabel, Annabelle,
Annette, Annata,
Annie, Anusia
Annunciata (*Feast of the
Blessed Mother*),
March 25
Anselina, April 21
Anselma
Antoinette, Feb. 28
Antoinetta, Antonetta
Antonia, Feb. 28
Antonina, Jan. 17
Anysia, Dec. 30
Anisia, Annice
Archangela, Feb. 13
Ardalia, April 14
Arlene (Helen), Aug. 18
Armella, Oct. 24
Arnoldine, March 14
Assunta, April 7
Auberta (Albert),
Nov. 15
Audrey, June 23
Aubrie
Augusta, March 27
Asta
Augustina, Aug. 28

Aulaire, Feb. 12
Aura, July 19
  Aurea, Goldie
Aurelia, Dec. 2
Austine, Aug. 28
Ava, April 29
Averil (Everild), July 9
Avida, May 7
Azelle, Dec. 6

B

Baptista, June 24
Barbara, Dec. 4
  Barba, Barbe, Barica, Barbora
Bartholomea, July 26
Bartillia, Jan. 3
Basila, Aug. 29
Basilia, Jan. 2
Basilissa, Jan. 9
  Basilla
Beata, March 8
Beatrice, July 29
  Bea, Beatrix
Belina, Feb. 19
  Belinda
Bellina, Sept. 9
Benedicta, March 21
  Benedeta, Beneta, Benita, Benite, Benoite, Benedetta
Benilda, June 15

Berenice, Oct. 4
  Bernice
Berina, Nov. 26
Bernadette, April 16
Bernarda (Bernard), Aug. 20
Bernardine, May 20
  Bernardina
Bertha, July 4
  Berthel, Bertel
Bertilla, Jan. 3
  Bertilia, Bertina
Betilda, Jan. 26
Beverley, May 7
  Beverly
Bibiana, Dec. 2
Birona, March 8
Blanche, July 5
  Bianca, Branca, Blanca, Blanch
Blandina, June 2
  Blandine
Bobilia, Oct. 16
Bonna, Oct. 16
  Bonita
Brenda (Brendan), May 16
Briana (Brian), March 22
Bridget (of Sweden, Oct. 8; of Ireland, Feb. 1)
  Bride, Brigette, Brigid, Brigitta

C

Cabrini (St. Frances Xavier), Dec. 22
Calista, Sept. 2
 Callista
Camelia, Sept. 16
 Camella
Camilla (Camillus), July 14
 Camila, Camille
Candia, Oct. 22
Candida, June 6
Canice, Oct. 11
Careme, Sept. 7
Carina, Nov. 7
Carisia, May 6
Carissima, Sept. 7
Carita, June 12
Carmel (*Our Lady of Mt. Carmel*), July 16
 Carmela, Carmelita, Carmelina, Carmen, Melita
Carmilla, March 23
Caroline (Charles), Nov. 4
 Carla, Carlen, Carleen, Carlene, Carletta, Carlina, Carlinna, Carlin, Carlita, Carilla, Carol, Carole, Carolina, Carrie, Charlene, Charlet, Cheryl
Casilda, April 9
Cassandra (Alexandra), May 18
Cassilda, April 9
Catalina, May 11
Catharine (Catherine), April 29
 Catana, Catania, Caterina, Cathleen, Katherine, Kathleen, Kathryn, Krina, Karen
Cazaria, Dec. 8
Cecilia, Nov. 22
 Caecilia, Cecile, Cecily, Celia, Celie, Celine, Cicile, Cisily
Celerina, Feb. 3
Celeste, April 16
 Celesta
Celestina, May 10
Celine, Oct. 21
Cella (Marcella), Jan. 31
Cera, Jan. 5
Cerenna, Nov. 15
Charity, Aug. 1
 Charissa, Cherry
Charlotte (Charles), Nov. 4
 Carlina, Carlota, Carlotta, Charlet, Cheryl

Charmaine (Charlemagne), Jan. 28
Chiara, Jan. 5
Christina, July 24
  Christa, Christabel, Christabelle, Christal, Christel, Christine, Cristina, Crystal, Kerstin
Cilinia, Oct. 21
Cineria, Oct. 29
Cinthia, Feb. 8
  Cynthia
Clare, Aug. 11
  Claire, Clara, Clareta, Clarice, Clarinda, Clarine, Claribel, Claribelle, Clarissa, Clarita, Chiara
Claudia, May 18
  Claudina, Claudine, Claudette
Clementina (Clement), Nov. 23
  Clemency, Clementine, Clemence
Cleopatra, Oct. 19
  Cleo
Colette, March 6
  Coletta, Collette
Colona, Dec. 31
Columba, Sept. 17
Columbina, May 22
  Columbine
Comelia, April 20
Conception *(Feast of our Blessed Mother: The Immaculate Conception)*, Dec. 8
  Concha, Conchita, Concetta
Concessa, April 8
Concordia, Aug. 13
Condita, Aug. 14
Conradine, Nov. 26
Constance, Sept. 19
  Constancia, Constantia
Consuelo *(Title of the Blessed Mother: Our Lady of Consolation)*
  Consuela, Consoleta
Cordelia, Oct. 22
  Cora, Corinne, Delia
Corintha, Aug. 8
Cornella, Sept. 16
  Cornelia
Corona, May 14
Cotilla, Jan. 23
Credola, May 13
Crescentia, June 15
  Crescencia
Cynthia, Feb. 8
Cyra, Aug. 3
Cyrena, Nov. 1
  Cyrenia

Cyria, June 5
Cyriaca, March 20
Cyriana, Nov. 1
Cyrilla, Feb. 14
  Cyrille

D

Daire, Nov. 2
Daisy (Margaret),
  June 10
Damaris, Oct. 4
  Demara
Damiana, Feb. 21
Daniela, July 21
  Danette, Danila,
  Danita, Danielle
Daphne, July 13
Daria, Oct. 25
  Darice
Datiana, May 31
Dauphine, Nov. 26
Davida, Dec. 29
  Davina, Vida
Deborah, Sept. 1
Deidre, Jan. 15
  Deirdre
Delia (Cordelia), Oct. 22
  Della
Delphine, Dec. 9
  Delfina, Delphina
Demetria, June 21
Denise (Denis), Oct. 9
  Denice, Denys
Desiree (Desiderius),
  May 23
  Desirata
Devota, Jan. 27
Diana, June 9
  Diane
Digna, Aug. 11
Dionysia, Dec. 12
  Dionetta, Dionisia,
  Diona
Dolores (*Title of the
  Blessed Mother: Our
  Lady of Sorrows*),
  Sept. 15
  Delores, Dolora,
  Dolorita, Deloris
Domaine, May 20
Dominica, Aug. 8
Donalda, July 15
Donata, Dec. 31
  Dona, Donna, Donora
Dorcas, Oct. 25
  Dorcea, Dorcia
Dorothy, Feb. 6
  Dora, Doralia,
  Doralice, Doralis,
  Doralise, Dore, Dorea,
  Dorelia, Dorena,
  Doretta, Dorette,
  Doria, Dorice,
  Dorinda, Dorinna,
  Doris, Dorissa, Dorita

Dorlisa, Dorna,
Dorothea
Drusilla, Sept. 22
　Drucilla
Dulcelina, Oct. 26
　Dulcea, Dulcia,
　Dulcie, Dulcina,
　Dulcyna
Dymphna, May 15

E

Eberta (Egbert), April 24
Edana, July 5
Edberga, June 15
Eden (Aedan), May 2
Edith, Sept. 16
　Edita, Editha, Edyth
Edmunda, Nov. 20
　Edmee, Edmonda
Edna (Edana), July 5
Edwarda, Oct. 13
　Edwardina,
　Edwardine
Edwina, Oct. 12
Egena, May 18
Eileen (Helen), Aug. 18
Elaine (Helen), Aug. 18
Eleanor, Aug. 16
　Eleanora, Eleanore,
　Eleonor, Lena, Nora
Elena, Nov. 4
Elenara, May 2
Elene (Helen), Aug. 18

Elevara, March 28
Elfrida, Dec. 8
　Elfreda
Elizabeth (Ann
　Seton, Jan. 4; of
　Hungary, Nov. 17;
　of Portugal, July 4)
　Beta, Beth, Betha,
　Betina, Betta, Bettina,
　Betty, Elisa, Elisabet,
　Elisabetta, Elise,
　Elisia, Elissa, Eliza,
　Elsa, Elsabet, Elsbeth,
　Elspeth, Elna, Elora,
　Helsa, Libby, Lisa,
　Lisbeth
Ella, Oct. 27
　Elletta, Ellette
Ellen (Helen), Aug. 18
Elma, April 15
Eloine (Eloi), Dec. 1
Eloise (Louise), Jan. 31
Elsie (Elizabeth), Nov. 5
Elvara, March 28
Elvira, Jan. 25
Emelia, May 23
Emeline, Oct. 27
Emerentiana, Jan. 23
　Emerentia
Emilda (Imelda), May 13
Emily, Sept. 19
　Emelin, Emelina,
　Emeline, Emelyn,

Emilie, Emmelia,
Emmeline
Emma, April 11
Enid, Aug. 1
Enora, April 12
Enrica (Henry), July 15
Enrika
Erena, May 5
Erica (Eric), May 18
Erika
Ermelinda, Oct. 29
Erma, Irma, Linda
Ernestina, Nov. 7
Erna, Ernesta,
Ernestine
Esperanza (Hope),
Aug. 1
Esperance
Esprite, Aug. 7
Estelle (Eustella),
April 30
Stella
Esther, July 1
Easter, Esthera,
Estra, Estrella,
Heather, Hester
Etha, May 5
Ethel, Jan. 12
Ethelina
Etta (Henry), July 15
Eugenia, Dec. 15
Eugenie
Eulalia, Feb. 12
Eulalie
Eunice, Oct. 28
Euphemia, March 20
Effie
Euralia, Dec. 10
Eurosia, June 25
Eustella, May 21
Eustelle
Euthalia, Aug. 27
Eutropia, Dec. 14
Eva, May 26
Evangelista, Sept. 16
Evangeline
Eve, Dec. 19
Aveline, Evelina,
Eveline, Evelien,
Evelyn, Lena, Lina

F

Fabia, Jan. 20
Fabiana, Fabienne
Fabiola, Dec. 27
Faila, March 3
Faina, May 18
Faith, Aug. 1
Fay, Faye, Fayette
Fanchette (Frances),
Oct. 4
Fanchon
Fara, April 3
Farica, July 18

Fatima, May 13
Faustina, Jan. 18
  Fausta, Faustine
Fedora (Theodora),
  April 1
Fedosia (Theodosia),
  April 2
Felicia, Oct. 5
  Felice, Felise, Felita
Felicity, March 7
Felipa (Philippa),
  Sept. 20
  Filipa, Felisa
Ferdinanda, May 30
  Fernanda, Fernande
Fidelia, March 23
Fidelity (Fidelis),
  April 24
Flavia, May 7
Flora, Nov. 24
  Florella, Floretta,
  Floria, Floris, Flossie
Florence, Nov. 10
  Florencia, Florentia,
  Florinda
Florentina, June 20
Floreta, Aug. 22
Florida, Aug. 29
Florina, May 1
Fonilla, Jan. 17
Fortuna, Feb. 22
  Fortune
Fortunata, Oct. 14
Fortunia, April 27
Franca, April 27
Frances (of Rome,
  March 9; Xavier
  Cabrini, Nov. 13;
  de Chantal, Dec. 12)
  Fanchette, Fanchon,
  Fanchonette, France,
  Francella, Francesca,
  Francine, Francisca
Francha, April 25
Freda (Fredrick),
  July 18
  Fredella, Frederica,
  Fredrika, Freida,
  Frida, Fritzi

G

Gabriella, Sept. 29
  Gabrielle, Gavrila,
  Gail, Gabriele,
  Gabriela
Gemina, Jan. 4
Gemma, April 11
Generosa, July 17
Genesia, Aug. 25
Genevieve, Jan. 3
  Genever, Genevra,
  Guinevere, Ginevra,
  Geneva
Genoise, Dec. 23
Gentile, Jan. 28

Georgia (George),
　April 23
　Georgetta, Georgette,
　Georgiana, Georgina,
　Georgine
Geralda, March 13
　Geraldina, Geraldine,
　Gerelda, Gerlinda,
　Giralda
Gerardine (Gerard),
　Oct. 16
Gerberta, Dec. 19
Germaine, June 15
Gertrude, Nov. 16
　Gertruda
Gilberta (Gilberte),
　Feb. 4
Gilda (Gildas), Jan. 29
Gisele, May 7
　Giselle, Gisella
Gladys, March 29
Gloria, May 10
　Gloriana, Glorianna,
　Glory
Glyceria, May 13
　Glitheria, Glycere
Godina, Feb. 15
Golinia, July 6
Goretti, July 6
Grace, July 5
　Gracia, Gratia,
　Gratiana
Graecina, June 16
Grata, May 1
Gredel (Margaret),
　June 10
Gregoria (Gregory),
　Jan. 2
Gresinda, July 25
Greta (Margaret),
　June 10
　Gretchen, Grethel,
　Grita
Guadalupe (*Famous Mexican Shrine of Our Lady of Guadalupe*), Dec. 12
Gudela (Gudelia),
　Sept. 29
Guenevere (Genevieve),
　Jan. 3
Guenna, Aug. 19
Guida (Guy), Sept. 12
Guilette (William),
　June 25
　Guillena
Gwen, July 5
　Gwenn
Gwendolene, Oct. 18
　Gwendolen, Gwendolin, Gwendoline,
　Gwendolyn

H

Hannah (Anne), July 26
Harolda (Harold),
　March 25

Harelda
Harriet (Henry), July 15
  Hariett, Harrietta
Hedwig, Oct. 16
  Hedda, Heidi
Helen, Aug. 18
  Aileen, Eileen,
  Elaine, Ellen, Ellin,
  Ellyn, Helena, Helene,
  Helenka, Ilona, Ilsa,
  Ilse, Lena, Lenora,
  Lenore, Leona,
  Leonora, Leonore,
  Pamela
Heliana, June 8
Heliena, April 20
Helmina (William),
  June 25
Heloise (Louise),
  Jan. 31
Helsa (Elizabeth),
  Nov. 5
Henrica (Henry),
  July 15
  Hendrica, Henrika,
  Henrita, Henryka,
  Henrietta, Henriette,
  Henrieta
Herena, Feb. 25
  Herene
Herenia, March 8
Herina, May 5
Herlanda, March 22
Hermana (Herman),
  April 7
  Hermandine,
  Hermine
Hermione, Sept. 4
  Hermia, Herminia
Hester (Esther), July 1
Hilaria, Jan. 13
Hilda, Nov. 17
Hildeburg, June 3
Hildegard, Sept. 17
  Hildegarda, Hildegarde, Hulda
Hiltrude, Sept. 27
Hirmina, Dec. 24
Honesta, Oct. 18
Honora, April 12
  Honore
Honorata, Jan. 11
Honoria, April 12
Hope, Aug. 1
  Esperanza, Nadine
Hortense, Jan. 11
Huberta (Hubert),
  Nov. 3
Huette (Hugh),
  April 29
  Huguetta, Hugette
Humbelina, Feb. 12
  Humbeline
Humility, May 22
Hyacinth, Jan. 30
  Hyacintha, Hyacinthe

I

Iacolyn (James), July 25
Ida, Sept. 4
   Idelle, Idette
Ignatia (Ignatius of Antioch, Oct. 17; Ignatius of Loyola, July 31)
   Ignacia
Illuminata, Nov. 29
Ilsa (Helen), Aug. 18
   Ilse, Ilona
Imelda, May 12
Immaculata (*Feast of the Immaculate Conception*), Dec. 8
Imogene (*Shrine of Blessed Virgin, at Imoge, France*) Sept. 8
   Imogen
Imperia, Sept. 6
Indica, May 9
Inez, Nov. 8
   Ines
Ingrid, July 1
   Inga
Innocensia (Holy Innocents), Dec. 28
   Innocentia
Iolana (Yolando), Dec. 28
Iolanda
Ionilla, Jan. 17
Irene, Oct. 20
   Irena, Irina
Irmina, Dec. 24
   Irma
Isabel, July 8
   Belita, Belle, Isabeau, Isabella, Isabelle, Isbel, Isobel
Isadora (Bishop and Doctor, April 4; farmer, May 14)
   Isidora
Ita, Jan. 15
Iva, Oct. 27
Ivanna (John), Dec. 27
Ivetta, Jan. 13
   Iveta, Ivette, Ivy
Ivona (Yvonne), May 19

J

Jacinta (Hyacinth), Jan. 30
   Jacintha, Jacinthe
Jacobina, Aug. 1
   Jacobia
Jacqueline (James), July 25
   Jacobella, Jacquetta, Jaculin, Jamesina, Jamesine

Jane, Dec. 12
  Janel, Janella, Janet,
  Janine, Janette,
  Janetta, Janice
  Johanna, Juanita,
  Jean, Jeanne,
  Jeanette, Jeanie,
  Jeanene, Jeanne
Janilla, Jan. 17
Januaria, Feb. 11
Jennifer (Winifred),
  Nov. 3
Jeonilla, Jan. 17
Jeremia, Jan. 21
Jeromina, Sept. 30
Jessica, May 24
  Jessie
Jill (Julia), May 22
Joan, May 30
  Joanine
Jobina (Job), May 10
Jocelyn, March 17
  Jocelin, Joceline,
  Josslyn
Jocunda, June 2
Joelene, July 13
Johanna, May 24
  Henchen
Jolenta, March 6
Joletta (Viola), May 3
  Jolietta
Jonella, Jan. 16
  Jonila

Josepha, Feb. 14
Josephine, Oct. 23
  Josephina, Giuseppa
Joy (Jucunda), July 27
Joyce (Jucunda), July 27
Juana, Dec. 8
Juanita, Aug. 21
Jucunda, July 27
Judith, Sept. 14
  Juditha, Judithe, Judy
Julia, May 22
  Julchen, Jule, Joli,
  Juliana, Juliane,
  Julianna, Julianne,
  Juliet, Julietta, Julita
Juliana, June 19
Julie, July 12
Juliette, May 18
Julitta, June 16
June (Junia), Nov. 14
Junella, Jan. 17
Junilla, Feb. 16
Justa, July 19
Justilla, Aug. 28
Justina, April 14
  Justine
Jutta, May 5

K

Karen (Catherine),
  Nov. 25
  Kara, Karena, Kalina,

Karin, Karina, Kasia,
Kassia, Katrina,
Katherine, Kathleen,
Katheryn, Kateri,
Katarina, Katinka,
Katrien
Karla (Charles), Nov. 4
Karoline, Nov. 4
Kayne, Oct. 8
Kerstin (Christiana),
  July 24
  Kirstie, Kisten,
  Kristina
Kilda, Nov. 1
Kinga, July 24

L

Lamberta, Sept. 17
  Lambertina,
  Lambertine
Landine, Jan. 16
  Landoline
Languida, Oct. 21
Latina, June 2
Laura, Oct. 19
  Laure, Laurena,
  Laurene, Laureen,
  Lauretta, Laurette,
  Laurine, Laurice,
  Lorita, Laurina, Lora,
  Loris, Laurinda
Laurentina, Oct. 8
  Laurentia

Laverne, Sept. 17
  LaVerne, Lavernne,
  Alvernia
Lea (Leah), March 22
Lee (Elizabeth), Nov. 5
Lelia, Aug. 11
Lelica, Feb. 12
  Lela
Lena (Helen), Aug. 18
  Lenchen, Lenia
Lene, Nov. 12
Lenora (Helen), Aug. 18
  Lenore, Leon, Leora,
  Lonie, Lora, Leonora
Leocardia, Dec. 9
Leona (Leo), April 11
  Leola, Leonie
Leonarda, Nov. 26
Leonice, March 1
Leonilla, Jan. 17
Leonita, March 1
  Leontina, Leontine
Leonora, June 3
Leopolda, April 2
  Leopoldina
Letitia, Dec. 25
  Leticia, Letty
Libaria, Oct. 8
Libera, Jan. 18
Liberta, Jan. 16
Liberty, Feb. 3
Libya, June 25
Liceria, May 11

Lidia, March 27
Lillian, July 27
  Lila, Lili, Lilah,
  Liley, Lilia, Lilis,
  Lilisa, Lillie, Lillien,
  Lillis
Lina, Aug. 18
Linda (Ermelinda),
  Oct. 29
Lisa (Elizabeth), Nov. 5
  Lise, Lisetta, Lisette,
  Lisbeth
Lois, Jan. 31
Lola, Jan. 31
Lolita (Dolores), Sept. 15
  Loleta
Lora (Laura), Oct. 19
Loraine (Laurentia),
  Oct. 8
Lorena, Aug. 10
  Lorna
Lorenza, Oct. 8
Loretta (*Shrine of Our Lady of Loretto, Italy*), Dec. 10
Louise, Jan. 31
  Lois, Lou, Louison,
  Lola
Lourdes, Feb. 11
Lucasta, June 27
Lucella, May 10
Luchina, Aug. 23
Lucia, Dec. 13
Luciana, May 18
Lucida, Jan. 3
Lucilla, June 29
  Lucille
Lucina, June 30
Lucinia, May 25
Lucosa, Sept. 28
Lucretia, Nov. 23
  Lucrece
Lucy, Dec. 13
  Lucasta, Luce, Lucilla,
  Lucia, Luciana, Lucie,
  Lucetta, Lucille,
  Lucina, Lucinda,
  Lucya
Ludmilla, Sept. 16
Ludovica, Jan. 31
Ludwina, April 14
  Lydwina
Luella (Louise-Ella),
  Aug. 25
  Louella
Luisa, Jan. 31
  Luise, Luiza
Lunette, Aug. 1
Lupe (Guadalupe),
  Dec. 12
Lydia, Aug. 3
  Lidia

M

Mabilia, Nov. 21
  Mabele, Mabelle,

Maybelle
Mabel (Mabilia), Nov. 21
Macrina, Jan. 14
Madalena (Magdalen),
 July 22
Madeleine, July 17
Madonna *(In honor of
 the Blessed Mother
 of our Lord Jesus
 Christ)*, Oct. 11
 Donna
Magda (Margaret),
 June 10
Magdalene (St. Mary
 Magdalene, July 22;
 de Pazzi, May 25)
 Madalene, Madeline,
 Madalyn, Madel,
 Madelon, Magdala,
 Magdalen, Mag-
 delaine, Malina,
 Marlina, Marlene
Magina, Dec. 3
Magita, Sept. 8
Magna, May 6
Maisie (Margaret),
 June 10
Majella, Oct. 16
 (St. Gerard Majella)
Malina, April 28
Mandie (Amanda),
 June 18
 Manda

Manon (Mary), Dec. 8
Manette
Manuelita (Manuel),
 June 17
Manuela
Marca (Mark), April 25
 Marcel, Marcele,
 Marcelle
Marcella, Jan. 31
 Marcel, Marcele,
 Marcelle, Marcellina
Marchell, Sept. 5
Marcia, March 3
Marciana, May 24
Marcina, June 8
Marella, May 21
Marga, April 6
Margaret, Nov. 16
 Madge, Magde, Marfa,
 Margareta, Margarita,
 Margarta, Margery,
 Margo, Margory,
 Marjory, Marjorie,
 Margala, Marguerite,
 Margola, Marsali,
 Maggie, Greta,
 Gretchen, Grethel,
 Gretel, Pearl, Maisie
Margaret Mary, Oct. 16
Maria Goretti, July 6
Marianna, April 17
 Mariana, Marianne
Marietta (Mary), Sept. 8

Marina, Feb. 12
Marita, March 16
Marsilia, April 8
Martana, Dec. 2
Martha, July 29
   Marta, Martel,
   Martella, Marthine
Martia, June 21
Martina, Jan. 30
   Martine,
Mary, Sept. 12
   Mara, Marea, Mare,
   Marella, Mair, Maire,
   Marise, Mariel, Mar-
   la, Maret, Marei, Mae,
   May, Maraline, Maria,
   Marie, Marian,
   Mariana, Mariane,
   Marien, Mari, Mari-
   ella, Marintha,
   Marion, Marionette,
   Marja, Marsia, Marya,
   Marusche, Mascha,
   Maureen, Maribel,
   Marilla, Marilyn,
   Mayme, Mollie, Molly
Matilda, March 14
   Machtilde, Mathilde,
   Matilde
Matutina, March 27
Maude, July 22
   Maud, Maudlin
Maura, July 13

Maure, Maureen
Mauritia, Sept. 22
Maxima, April 8
Maximilla, Feb. 19
Maxine (Maximillian),
   Oct. 12
Mayra, July 28
   May
Mazota, Dec. 23
Mechtilde, Nov. 16
Melania, Dec. 31
   Melanie, Melani,
   Melany
Melinda (Ermelinda),
   Oct. 29
   Melina
Mercedes (*In honor of
   Our Lady of Mercy*),
   Sept. 24
   Merced, Mercy,
   Merry
Merita, Sept. 22
Messina, April 19
Michele (Michael),
   Sept. 29
   Michelle, Michon,
   Miguela, Michaela,
   Michelina
Mildred, July 13
   Millie, Milly
Milissa, March 16
   Milice
Mina (Wilhelmina),

June 25
Minette
Minerva, Oct. 25
Miriam (Mary), Sept. 12
Mitrina, Aug. 8
Modesta, Nov. 4
   Modesty
Modwenna, July 5
Moira (Myron), Aug. 8
Monessa, Sept. 4
Monica, Aug. 27
   Mona, Monique
Monice, April 16
Monna, Nov. 26
Montana, May 25
Murenna, May 26
Muriel (Myron), Aug. 8
   Mergl, Meriel, Myra
Myra (Myron), Aug. 8
   Mira, Mirilla, Myrilla
Myrtle (Murial), Aug. 8

N

Nadine (Hope), Aug. 1
   Nada
Nana, Nov. 22
Nancy (Anne), July 26
   Nanette, Nanon,
   Nanna, Nanelia
Narcissa, March 18
Natalie, July 27
   Natalia, Natasha,
   Natica, Natalina
Nathania (Nathaniel), Aug. 24
Nell (Cornelia), March 31
   Neala, Nelia, Nella,
   Nelle, Nellis, Nelena
Nessa, July 10
   Nessia
Neysa (Agnes), Jan. 21
Nicea (Nichelle), Aug. 29
Niceta, July 24
Nicolette (Nicholas), Dec. 6
   Nichola, Nicolina
Nina (Anne), July 26
   Ninetta, Ninon, Nanon
Nirilla, May 21
Nita (Joan), May 30
Noel (*Nativity of our Lord*), Dec. 25
   Noella, Nielle
   Noelita
Nona, Oct. 31
Nonna, Aug. 5
Norah (Honora), April 12
   Nora, Noreen, Norena,
   Norine
Norma, Aug. 5
Norrice, Aug. 25

Norvella, April 12
Nunciata (*Feast of the Annunciation*), March 25
    Annunciata

O

Octavia, April 15
Odella, Feb. 12
Odilia, Dec. 13
    Odile, Adilia
Ola (Olaf), July 29
Olga, July 11
    Helga
Olive, June 10
    Oliva, Olivia
Olympia, Dec. 17
Onesta (Honesta), Oct. 18
Onora (Honora), April 12
Oranda, Sept. 15
Orlanda (Orlando), May 20
Othilia, Dec. 13
    Ottilia

P

Pacifica, March 24
Pamela (Helen), Aug. 18
Pandonia, Aug. 26
Patience, May 1
Patricia, Aug. 25
    Patrice, Tricia, Tracy
Paula, Jan. 25
    Pala, Poila, Paule, Paulina, Pauline, Paulette, Paulita
Penelope (Irene), Oct. 20
Perpetua, March 7
Persia, Feb. 8
Petrine (Peter), June 29
    Petrina, Petra
Petronilla, May 31
    Perette, Pernell, Petrina
Philea, Nov. 17
Philene (Philo), April 25
Philippa, May 1
    Philippina, Pippa
Philomena, Aug. 11
    Filomena
Phoebe, Sept. 3
    Phebe
Pierrette (Peter), June 29
Placida, Oct. 11
Polonia (Appolonia), Feb. 9
    Pollyanna
Pontiana, Feb. 27
Prima, Feb. 9
Primeva, Feb. 11

Principia, May 11
Prisca, Nov. 18
Priscilla, Jan. 16
  Pricilla
Prudence, May 19
  Prudentia, Prue
Pura *(From the Feast of the Purification of the Blessed Mother)*, Feb. 2

Q

Quieta, Nov. 28
Quinta, Feb. 8
  Quintina
Quintilla, March 19
Quirilla, May 15
Quiteria, June 4

R

Rachel, Sept. 2
  Rachela, Rachele, Rachelle
Radiana, Aug. 13
Ragnild, July 28
Rainalda, July 16
Raingarda, Jan. 26
Ramona (Raymond), Jan. 23
Raphaela, Sept. 2
  Rafaela
Ravenna, July 23
Raymonda, Jan. 7
Rebecca
  Reba
Regina, Aug. 22
  Regia, Reine, Reinette, Reina, Reyne
Renata, Sept. 26
  Renee, Rena
Renelda, March 22
Reyne, Sept. 7
  Rhonda
Richarda, April 3
Richelia, Feb. 1
  Richella
Rita, May 22
  Reta
Ritza, Aug. 30
Roberta, Sept. 17
  Robina, Robenetta, Robenette, Robinia
Roderica, March 13
Rogata, May 31
Rolanda, Sept. 15
Rolenda, May 13
  Rollande, Rollende
Roma, Jan. 21
Romana, April 6
  Romaine, Romayne
Romula, July 23
Ronalda, Aug. 20
Rosalia, Sept. 4
Rosalind, June 11
Rosamond, April 3

Rosaria *(Feast of Our Lady of the Rosary)*, Oct. 7
Rose, Aug. 23
  Rosabel, Rosabelle, Rosalba, Rosalia, Rosalie, Rosalind, Rosalinde, Rosaleen, Rosaline, Roseta, Rosetta, Rosette, Rosina, Rosita, Rosalyn, Rosamond, Rosamund, Roanna, Rosel, Roselle, Rosemare, Rosetta,
Roseline, Jan. 17
Rosena, March 17
Roseanne (Rose-Anne), July 26
Rosseline, June 11
  Rosalind
Roxanna, May 22
  Roxanne, Roxane
Ruby (Robert), May 13
  Rubetta
Rudolpha (Rudolph), July 27
  Rudolfa
Ruth, Sept. 1

S

Sabela, Dec. 18
Sabina, Aug. 29
  Sabine
Sacha (Alexander), Feb. 26
Sadie (Sarah), Dec. 23
Salome, June 29
Salomea, Nov. 17
Samina, June 2
Samuela, Aug. 20
Sancha, March 13
Sancta, Aug. 16
Sandra (Alexander), May 18
Santina, May 2
Sara, Dec. 10
Sarah, Dec. 23
  Sadie, Sarita
Sarapia, Aug. 29
Sarona, May 28
Satira, May 10
Savina, May 7
Scholastica, Feb. 10
Sebastiana, Jan. 20
Secunda, Jan. 15
  Secundina
Selina (Celestina), Oct. 21
  Selena, Selene, Celine
Selma (Anselm), April 21
Senorina, April 22
Seraphina, July 29
  Seraphine, Serafine

Serapia, July 29
Serena, Aug. 16
Sevilla (Sibylla),
    March 19
Sharon (*Rose of Sharon,
a title of the Blessed
Mother*)
Sheila (Cecilia), Nov. 22
  Sheelar, Sheela
Sibylla (Sibyllina),
    March 23
  Sibelle, Sibille, Sibil,
  Sibley, Sibyl, Sibylle,
  Sibylla, Sybilla, Sybila
Sidonia, Aug. 21
  Sidonie
Silva, Dec. 15
Simona, Oct. 28
  Simonette, Simone
Sirina, Aug. 26
Sophia, Sept. 30
  Sofia, Sonia, Sonya,
  Sophie
Speranza (Hope),
    Aug. 1
Stasia (Anastasia),
    Dec. 25
  Stacie
Stella, July 10
Stephanie, Jan. 16
  Stefana, Stefanie
Successa, March 27

Sunniva, July 8
  Sunnifa
Susanna, Aug. 11
  Susan, Susanne,
  Susannah, Suzanna,
  Suzanne, Suzette
  Suzette
Sylvia, July 10
  Silvania, Silvia, Silvie,
  Sylwyn
Symphrosia, July 18
Syria, June 8

T

Tama, Oct. 11
Tamasine (Thomas),
    Dec. 21
Tarasia, Sept. 3
Tarcisia, Aug. 15
Tarsilla, Dec. 24
Tarsitia, Jan. 15
  Tharsilla
Tatiana, Jan. 12
Terentiana, July 10
  Teresita
Teresa (of Avila),
    Oct. 15
  Teresina, Terisia,
  Tess, Tessa, Tessie,
  Tracy, Tressa, Terecita
Thadine (Thaddeus),
    Oct. 28

Thea, July 25
Thecla, Sept. 23
   Tecla, Tekla, Thecle, Thekla
Theda (Theodora), April 1
Thelma (Anthelmius), June 26
Theodora, April 1
Theodosia, April 2
Theresa, Oct. 1
   Therese, Theresia
Thomasina (Thomas, Apostle, July 3; Aquinas, Jan. 28; Becket, Dec. 29; More, June 22)
   Tomasa, Thomasia, Thomasine
Tilda (Matilda), March 14
Timothea, Jan. 26
Titiana, July 17
Trina (Catherine), April 30
   Trine, Trinette
Trophe (Eutropia), Dec. 14
Trude (Gertrude), Nov. 16
   Trudel, Trudy

U

Ulrica (Ulric), July 4
   Ulrika, Ulrique
Una (Winifred), Nov. 3
Urania, May 28
Urbana, May 17
Ursa, Oct. 26
Ursula, Oct. 21
   Ursel, Ursele
Ursulina (Bl.), April 7

V

Valentia, July 25
   Valentine, Valentina
Valeria, April 28
   Valerie
Valerina, Nov. 15
Vanessa (Esther), July 1
Vanora, Jan. 3
Vaudree, May 5
Vaune, Nov. 9
Vendreda (Winifred), June 5
Venetia (Beatrice), July 29
   Venice
Venisa, July 12
Vera, Jan. 24
Verbetta, Sept. 16
Verdiana, Feb. 1
Verena, Sept. 1

Verona, Aug. 29
Veronica, July 12
  Verenice, Veron, Venise
Vestina, July 17
  Vesta
Vevette (Genevieve), Jan. 3
Vicentia (Vincent), April 5
Victorina, July 28
  Victorine
Victory, Dec. 23
  Victoria, Victoire, Victoire
Vidette (David), Dec. 29
  Vida
Vigilia, June 26
Vincentia, June 4
Viola, May 3
  Violante, Violet, Violetta, Violette
Virginia *(In honor of the Blessed Virgin)*,
Vivian, Dec. 2
  Viva, Vivien, Vivienne
Vladislawa (Ladislaus), June 27

W

Walburga, Feb. 25

Wanda (Wando), April 17
Wilfreda, Sept. 9
  Wilfrida
Wilhelmina (William), Jan. 10
  Willa, Wileen, Willabel, Willabelle, Wilhelmine, Wilette, Williamina, Wilma, Helmina
Winifred, Nov. 3
  Winfreda

X

Xantippa, Sept. 23
  Xantippe
Xaverie (Xavier), Dec. 3
Xene, Jan. 24
Xenia, Sept. 23
  Zenia
Ximena (Simon), Oct. 28
Xina (Christina), July 24

Y

Yoland, April 23
  Yolaine
Yolanda, Nov. 18
  Yolande, Yolanthe, Yolette
Ysabeau (Isabel), July 8

Ysabel
Yvette, Jan. 13
Yvonne, Aug. 21

Z

Zandra (Alexandra), May 18
Zanetta (Joanna), May 24
Zelina (Soline), Oct. 17
Zenia, Sept. 23
Zenobia, Oct. 30
Zita, April 27
Zoe, May 2
Zona, Feb. 9
Zoa

Patron Saints

Long established custom and devotion have designated certain saints as patrons and protectors for those in particular professions or occupations as well as others to be invoked in times of special need.

A

ABANDONED CHILDREN . . . . . St. Jerome Emiliani
ACCOUNTANTS . . . . St. Matthew
ACTORS . . . . St. Genesius
ADVERTISING . . . . St. Bernardine
ALPINISTS . . . . St. Bernard
ALTAR BOYS . . . . St. John Berchmans
AMERICA . . . . Mary, Immaculate Conception
AMMUNITION WORKERS . . . . St. Barbara
AMPUTEES . . . . St. Anthony
ANESTHESIOLOGISTS . . . . St. Rene
ANIMALS . . . . St. Francis of Assisi
APOSTLESHIP OF PRAYER . . . . . St. Francis Xavier
APOTHECARIES . . . . St. Raphael

APPLE ORCHARDS	St. Charles Borromeo
ARCHAEOLOGISTS	St. Helen
ARCHERS	St. Sebastian
ARCHITECTS	St. Barbara
ARGENTINA	Our Lady of Luzon
ARMENIA	St. Gregory Illuminator
ARMORERS	St. Sebastian
ARROWSMITHS	St. Sebastian
ART DEALERS	St. John the Evangelist
ARTHRITIS	St. James
ARTILLERY	St. Barbara
ARTISTS	St. Luke
ASIA MINOR	St. John the Evangelist
ASTRONOMERS	St. Dominic
ATHLETES	St. Sebastian
AUSTRALIA	St. Francis Xavier
AUSTRIA	St. Colman, St. Stephen
AUTHORS	St. Paul, Apostle; St. Francis de Sales
AVIATORS	St. Joseph Cupertino, St. Theresa, Our Lady of Loretto

B

BACHELORS	St. Christopher
BAKERS	St. Nicholas, St. Meingold
BANKERS	St. Matthew
BARBERS	Sts. Cosmas and Damian
BARREN WOMEN	St. Felicitas, St. Anthony
BASKET MAKERS	St. Anthony, Abbot
BATTLE	St. Michael
BEEKEEPERS	St. Ambrose
BEGGARS	St. Alexis
BELGIUM	St. Joseph

BELL FOUNDERS	St. Agatha
BELT MAKERS	St. Alexis
BIRDS	St. Francis of Assisi
BLACK CATHOLIC MISSIONS	St. Peter Claver
BLACKS	St. Martin de Porres
BLACKSMITHS	St. James
BLINDNESS	St. Odillia, St. Lawrence the Illuminator
BOATMEN	St. Julian Hospitallar
BODILY ILLS	Our Lady of Lourdes
BOHEMIA	St. Wenceslaus
BOOKBINDERS	St. Peter Celestine, St. Sebastian
BOOKKEEPERS	St. Matthew
BOOK SELLERS	Sts. John of God, John Evangelist
BORNEO	St. Francis Xavier
BOY SCOUTS	St. George
BRASS WORKERS	St. Barbara
BRAZIL	St. Peter of Alcantara, Immaculate Conception
BREWERS	St. Nicholas
BRIDES	St. Dorothy
BRIDGE BUILDERS	St. Peter
BRUISES	St. Amalberga
BRUSH MAKERS	St. Anthony, Abbot
BUILDERS	St. Vincent Ferrer, St. Barbara
BUS DRIVERS	St. Christopher
BUTCHERS	St. Hadrian, St. Anthony, Abbot

C

CAB DRIVERS	St. Fiacre
CABINET MAKERS	St. Anne
CANADA	St. Anne, St. Joseph

CANCER	St. Peregrine, James Salamoni
CARPENTERS	St. Joseph
CASKET MAKERS	St. Stephen
CATECHISTS	St. Robert Bellarmine, St. Charles Borromeo
CATHOLIC ACTION	St. Francis of Assisi
CATHOLIC UNIVERSITIES	St. Thomas Aquinas
CATTLE DISEASES	St. Sebastian
CAVALRY	St. George
CEMETERY WORKERS	St. Anthony
CEYLON	St. Lawrence
CHARITY	St. Vincent de Paul
CHASTITY	St. Agnes
CHEMICAL INDUSTRIES	Sts. Cosmas and Damian
CHILDREN	St. Nicholas
CHILE	St. James, Our Lady of Mt. Carmel
CHINA	St. Francis Xavier, St. Joseph
CHOIR BOYS	Holy Innocents, St. Dominic Savio
CIVIL SERVANTS	St. Thomas More
CLERGY	St. Charles Borromeo
CLERICS	St. Gabriel of the Sorrowful Mother
CLOCK MAKERS	St. Peter
CLOTH DYEING	St. Lydia
CLOTHING INDUSTRY	St. Paul the Hermit
COLIC	St. Charles Borromeo
COLOMBIA	St. Peter Claver
COMEDIANS	St. Genesius
COMMUNICATIONS MEDIA	St. Gabriel the Archangel

COMPOSERS	St. Cecilia
COMPOSITORS	St. John the Evangelist
CONFECTIONERS	St. Joseph
CONFESSORS	St. Francis de Sales
CONGO	Our Lady, Queen of Nations
CONVERSION AND BAPTISM	St. John the Baptist
CONVULSIONS IN CHILDREN	St. Scholastica
COOKS	St. Martha, St. Lawrence
COOPERS	St. Nicholas
COPPERSMITHS	St. Maurus
COUNSEL	Holy Spirit
COURT WORKERS	St. Thomas More
CRAMPS	St. Maurice
CRIPPLES	St. Giles
CZECHOSLOVAKIA	St. John Nepomucene, St. Wenceslaus

D

DAIRY WORKERS	St. Brigid
DANCERS	St. Genesius
DEAF	St. Francis de Sales
DENMARK	St. Ansgar
DENTISTS	St. Appolonia
DESPERATE SITUATIONS	St. Rita, St. Jude
DIABOLICAL POSSESSION	St. Bruno
DIETICIANS	St. Martha
DOCTORS	St. Luke
DOG BITES	St. Hubert
DOG FANCIERS	St. Roque
DOMESTIC ANIMALS	St. Anthony

DOMESTIC SERVANTS	St. Martha, St. Zita
DOUBT	St. Joseph
DRUGGIST	St. Raphael the Archangel, Sts. Cosmas and Damian
DYING	St. Joseph

E

EAST INDIES	St. Thomas, apostle
ECUADOR	Sacred Heart
EDITORS	St. John Bosco
EMIGRANTS	St. Frances Xavier Cabrini
ENEMIES OF RELIGION	St. Sebastian
ENGINEERS	St. Ferdinand, St. Joseph
ENGLAND	St. George
ENGRAVERS	St. John the Evangelist
ENLIGHTENMENT	Our Lady of Good Counsel
EPILEPSY	St. Genesius
ETHIOPIA	St. Frumentius
EXPECTANT MOTHERS	St. Elizabeth, St. Gerard
EYE DISEASES	St. Raphael the Archangel
EYES	St. Lucy

F

FAITH IN THE BLESSED SACRAMENT	St. Anthony
FALSELY ACCUSED	St. Raymond Nonnatus, St. Gerard
FAMILIES	St. Joseph

FAMILY HARMONY	St. Dymphna
FARMERS	St. Isidore
FEAR OF THE LORD	Holy Spirit
FEVER	St. Peter
FINLAND	St. Henry of Upsala
FIRE	St. Francis of Assisi
FIREMEN	St. Florian
FIRE PREVENTION	St. Catherine of Siena
FIREWORKS	St. Barbara
FIRST COMMUNICANTS	St. Tarcisius, Bl. Imelda, St. Pius X
FISHERMEN	St. Andrew, St. Peter
FLOODS	St. Columban
FLORISTS	St. Dorothy
FLOUR INDUSTRY WORKERS	St. Arnulph
FLYERS	St. Joseph Cupertino, Our Lady of Loretto
FOOT TROUBLE	St. Peter
FORTIFICATIONS	St. Barbara
FORTITUDE	Holy Spirit
FOUNDLINGS	Holy Innocents
FRANCE	St. Joan of Arc
FRENZY	St. Peter
FULLERS	St. James the Less
FUNERAL DIRECTORS	St. Dismas

G

GALL STONES	St. Liberius
GAMBLING, UNCONTROLLED	St. Bernardine
GARDENERS	St. Dorothy, St. Sebastian

GERMANY	St. Boniface, St. Michael
GIRL SCOUTS	St. Agnes
GLANDULAR DISORDERS	St. Cadoc
GLASS INDUSTRY	St. Luke
GLAZIERS	St. Mark
GOLDSMITHS	St. Anastasius, St. Luke
GOUT	St. Andrew
GRANDMOTHERS	St. Anne
GRAVE DIGGERS	St. Anthony
GREECE	St. Nicholas
GREETING CARDS INDUSTRY	St. Valentine
GROCERS	St. Michael
GUNNERS	St. Barbara

H

HAPPY DEATH	St. Joseph
HARDWARE	St. Sebastian
HATTERS	St. James the Less, St. Severus
HAZARDS OF TRAVELING	St. Christopher
HEADACHES	St. Denis
HEALING OF WOUNDS	St. Rita
HEART AILMENTS	St. John of God
HERNIA	St. Conrad
HESITATION	St. Joseph
HOLLAND	St. Willibrord
HOME BUILDERS	Our Lady of Loretto
HOPELESS CASES	St. Jude
HORSEMEN	St. Anne
HOSPITAL WORKERS	St. Vincent de Paul

HOSPITALS	St. Camillus, St. John of God, St. Vincent de Paul
HOTEL INDUSTRY WORKERS	St. Amandus
HOUSEKEEPERS	St. Martha, St. Anne
HOUSEWIVES	St. Anne
HUNGARY	St. Stephen of Hungary, Our Lady
HUNTERS	St. Eustace, St. Hubert

I

IMMIGRANTS	St. Frances Xavier Cabrini
IMPENITENCE	St. Barbara
IMPULSIVE GAMBLING	St. Bernardine
INFANTRYMEN	St. Maurice
INN KEEPERS	St. Julian the Hospitaller, St Armand
INSANITY	St. Dymphna
INVALIDS	St. Roque
IRELAND	St. Columba, St. Patrick
IRON MONGERS	St. Sebastian
ITALY	St. Catherine of Siena

J

JAPAN	St. Peter Baptist
JESUIT ORDER	St. Ignatius of Loyola
JEWELLERS	St. Eligius
JOURNALISTS	St. Paul, Apostle; St. Francis de Sales
JUDGES	St. Ives
JURORS	St. Catherine of Alexandria

K

KNIGHTS	St. Michael
KNOWLEDGE	Holy Spirit

L

LABORERS	St. James
LACE MAKERS	St. Francis of Assisi
LAMP MAKERS	Our Lady of Loretto
LAST SACRAMENTS	St. Stanislaus
LATIN AMERICA	St. Rose of Lima
LAWYERS	St. Thomas More, St. Ives
LEAD WORKERS	St. Sebastian
LEARNING	St. Margaret of Scotland, St. Ambrose
LEPERS	St. Vincent de Paul
LIBERAL ARTS	St. Catherine of Bologna
LIBRARIANS	St. Jerome
LIGHTNING	St. Barbara
LITHOGRAPHERS	St. John the Evangelist
LITHUANIA	St. Casimir
LOCKSMITHS	St. Dunstan
LONELINESS	St. Rita
LONG LIFE	St. Peter
LOST ARTICLES	St. Anthony
LOVERS	St. Raphael
LUMBAGO	St. Lawrence
LUNATICS	St. Dymphna
LUNGS AND CHEST	St. Bernardine

M

MACHINISTS	St. Hubert
MAIDS	St. Zita
MALL SERVERS	St. John Berchmans
MANUAL LABORERS	St. James the Greater
MARBLE WORKERS	St. Clement I
MARINERS	St. Michael
MARRIED COUPLES	St. Joseph
MASONS	St. Peter
MASS MEDIA	St. Gabriel the Archangel
MATHEMATICIANS	St. Hubert
MEDICAL SOCIAL WORKERS	St. John Regis
MEDICAL TECHNOLOGISTS	St. Albert
MENTAL ILLNESS	St. Dymphna
MERCHANTS	St. Amand, St. Francis of Assisi
MESSENGERS	St. Gabriel the Archangel
METAL WORKERS	St. Hubert
MEXICO	Our Lady of Guadalupe
MILLERS	St. Arnulph
MINERS	St. Piron, St. Barbara
MISSIONERS	St. Francis Xavier
MISSIONS	St. Theresa, St. Francis Xavier
MONASTICS	St. Benedict
MONKS	St. Benedict
MORTICIANS	St. Joseph of Arimathea
MOTHERS	St. Gerard, St. Anne
MOTORCYCLISTS	Our Lady of the Miraculous Medal
MOTORISTS	St. Christopher
MOUNTAIN CLIMBERS	St. Bernard
MUSICIANS	St. Cecilia

N

NAIL MAKERS	St. Claude
NAVIGATORS	Our Lady, Star of the Sea
NCCW	Our Lady of Good Counsel
NEEDLE WORKERS	St. Francis of Assisi
NERVES	St. Dymphna
NET MAKERS	St. Peter
NEW ZEALAND	St. Francis Xavier
NEWBORN BABIES	St. Brigid
NORWAY	St. Olaf
NOTARIES	St. Luke, St. Ives
NUNS	St. Brigid
NURSES	St. Raphael, St. John of God, St. Camillus de Lellis

O

OBSTETRICIANS	St. Raymond Nonnatus
OLD MAIDS	St. Andrew
ORATORS	St. John Chrysostom
ORGAN MAKERS	St. Cecilia
ORPHANS	St. Jerome Emiliani, St. Louise

P

PAINTERS	St. Luke
PAPER MAKERS	St. John the Evangelist
PARATROOPERS	St. Michael
PARISH PRIESTS	St. John Vianney

PAWN BROKERS	St. Nicholas
PEACE	St. Norbert
PEASANTS	St. Lucy
PEDDLERS	St. Lucy
PENCIL MAKERS	St. Thomas Aquinas
PERIL AT SEA	St. Michael
PERU	St. Joseph
PHILIPPINES	St. Rose of Lima, Immaculate Heart of Mary
PHILOSOPHERS	St. Justin Martyr, St. Catherine
PHYSICIANS	St. Raphael, Sts. Cosmas and Damian, St. Luke
PIETY	Holy Spirit
PILGRIMS	St. Alexius, St. James
PIONEERS	St. Joseph
PLAGUE	St. Roque
PLASTERERS	St. Bartholomew
POETS	St. Cecilia
POISONING	St. Benedict
POLAND	St. Casimir, St. Stanislaus
POLICEMEN	St. Michael
POLIO	St. Margaret Mary
POOR	St. Lawrence, St. Anthony, St. Martin de Porres
PORTERS	St. Christopher
PORTUGAL	St. Francis Borgia
POSTAL EMPLOYEES	St. Gabriel the Archangel
POTTERS	St. Sebastian
POULTRY RAISERS	St. Brigid
PRESS	St. Paul, Apostle; St. Francis de Sales
PRIESTS	St. John Vianney

PRINTERS .... St. John the Evangelist
PRISONS .... St. Joseph Cafasso
PRISONERS ...... St. Barbara, St. Vincent de Paul
PUBLIC RELATIONS .... St. Bernardine
PUBLISHERS .... St. Paul, Apostle; St. John
the Evangelist

R

RACQUET MAKERS .... St. Sebastian
RADIO WORKERS .... St. Gabriel
RADIOLOGISTS .... St. Michael
RAIN .... St. Scholastica
RANCHERS .... St. Isidore
REFUGEES .... St. Alban
RETREATS .... St. Ignatius of Loyola
RHEUMATISM .... St. James the Greater
RUSSIA .... St. Boris, St. Nicholas, St. Andrew

S

SADDLERS .... St. Lucy
SAFE JOURNEY .... St. Raphael
SAILORS .... St. Brendan, Our Lady Star
of the Sea, St. Michael, St. Cuthbert
SALESMEN .... St. Lucy
SCHOLARS .... St. Thomas Aquinas
SCHOOLS .... St. Thomas Aquinas
SCIENTISTS .... St. Albert
SCOTLAND .... St. Andrew
SCRIBES .... St. Catherine
SCULPTORS .... St. Claude, St. Luke
SEAFARERS .... St. Michael

SECRETARIES	St. Catherine
SEMINARIANS	St. Charles Borromeo
SERVANTS	St. Martha
SERVICE WOMEN	St. Joan of Arc
SHEEP RAISERS	St. Raphael
SHIP BUILDERS	St. Peter
SHOEMAKERS	St. Crispin
SICILY	St. Nicholas
SICK	St. Camillus de Lellis
SILVERSMITHS	St. Andronicus
SINGERS	St. Gregory the Great, St. Cecilia
SKATERS	St. Lidwina
SKIERS	St. Bernard
SKIN DISEASES	St. Roch, St. Peregrine
SNAKEBITE	St. Patrick
SOLDIERS	St. Sebastian, St. Ignatius of Loyola, St. George
SOLITARY DEATH	St. Francis of Assisi
SOUTH AMERICA	St. Rose of Lima
SPAIN	St. James the Great
SPELEOLOGISTS	St. Benedict
SPINSTERS	St. Catherine
SPIRITUAL DIRECTORS	St. Charles Borromeo
SPIRITUAL HELP	St. Vincent de Paul
STAINED GLASS WORKERS	St. Mark
STATIONERS	St. Peter
STENOGRAPHERS	St. Catherine
STOCKBROKERS	St. Matthew
STOMACH TROUBLE	St. Charles Borromeo
STONE MASONS	St. Barbara, St. Stephen, St. Sebastian
STONECUTTERS	St. Clement I

STONEWORKERS	St. Stephen
STORMS	St. Theodore, St. Barbara
STUDENTS	St. Thomas Aquinas
SUDDEN DEATH	St. Barbara
SURGEONS	Sts. Cosmas and Damian, St. Luke
SWEDEN	St. Brigit
SWITZERLAND	St. Antiochus, St. Nicholas
SWORDSMITHS	St. Dunstan, St. Maurice

T

TAILORS	St. Homobonus, St. John the Baptist
TANNERS	St. Simon Stock, St. James
TAXMEN	St. Matthew
TEACHERS	St. Gregory, St. Francis de Sales St. Catherine of Alexandria, St. John Baptist de la Salle
TELEGRAPH	St. Gabriel
TELEPHONE WORKERS	St. Gabriel
TELEVISION	St. Clare of Assisi
TEMPTATION	St. Michael
TERTIARIES	St. Elizabeth of Hungary, St. Louis X
THEOLOGIANS	St. Augustine, St. Thomas Aquinas
THROAT	St. Blase
TINSMITHS	St. Joseph of Arimathea
TONGUE	St. Catherine
TOOTHACHE	St. Apollonia
TOY MAKERS	St. Claude
TRAVEL	St. Paul, Apostle; St. Christopher

TRUCK DRIVERS	St. Christopher
TUBERCULOSIS	St. Theresa of Lisieux
TUMORS	St. Rita

U

ULCERS	St. Charles Borromeo
UNCONTROLLED GAMBLING	St. Bernardine
UNDERSTANDING	Holy Spirit
UNDERTAKERS	St. Sebastian
UNITED STATES	Immaculate Conception
UNIVERSAL CHURCH	St. Joseph

V

VANITY	St. Rose of Lima
VETERINARIANS	St. James
VIRGINS	St. Agnes, St. Joan of Arc, the Virgin Mary
VOCALISTS	St. Cecilia
VOCATIONS	St. Alphonsus

W

"WAC"	St. Joan of Arc
"WAVES"	St. Joan of Arc
WALES	St. David
WAREHOUSES	St. Barbara
WATCHMEN	St. Peter of Alcantara
WEAVERS	St. Anastasia, St. Barnabas
WEST INDIES	St. Gertrude

WHEELWRIGHTS	St. Catherine of Alexandria
WIDOWS	St. Louise
WILD ANIMALS	St. Blase
WINEMAKERS	St. Francis Xavier
WISDOM	Holy Spirit
WOLVES	St. Peter
WOMEN IN LABOR	St. Anne
WOOLWORKERS	St. Bernardine
WRITERS	St. Paul, Apostle; St. John the Evangelist

Y

YACHTSMEN	Our Lady Star of the Sea
YOUTH	St. Aloysius Gonzaga, St. Gabriel of the Sorrowful Mother, St. John Berchmans, St. Dominic Savio, St. Maria Goretti

Pauline
BOOKS & MEDIA

The Daughters of St. Paul operate book and media centers at the following addresses. Visit, call or write the one nearest you today, or find us on the World Wide Web, www.pauline.org

CALIFORNIA
3908 Sepulveda Blvd, Culver City, CA 90230 310-397-8676
5945 Balboa Avenue, San Diego, CA 92111 858-565-9181
46 Geary Street, San Francisco, CA 94108 415-781-5180

FLORIDA
145 S.W. 107th Avenue, Miami, FL 33174 305-559-6715

HAWAII
1143 Bishop Street, Honolulu, HI 96813 808-521-2731
Neighbor Islands call: 800-259-8463

ILLINOIS
172 North Michigan Avenue, Chicago, IL 60601 312-346-4228

LOUISIANA
4403 Veterans Blvd, Metairie, LA 70006 504-887-7631

MASSACHUSETTS
885 Providence Hwy, Dedham, MA 02026 781-326-5385

MISSOURI
9804 Watson Road, St. Louis, MO 63126 314-965-3512

NEW JERSEY
561 U.S. Route 1, Wick Plaza, Edison, NJ 08817 732-572-1200

NEW YORK
150 East 52nd Street, New York, NY 10022 212-754-1110
78 Fort Place, Staten Island, NY 10301 718-447-5071

PENNSYLVANIA
9171-A Roosevelt Blvd, Philadelphia, PA 19114 215-676-9494

SOUTH CAROLINA
243 King Street, Charleston, SC 29401 843-577-0175

TENNESSEE
4811 Poplar Avenue, Memphis, TN 38117 901-761-2987

TEXAS
114 Main Plaza, San Antonio, TX 78205 210-224-8101

VIRGINIA
1025 King Street, Alexandria, VA 22314 703-549-3806

CANADA
3022 Dufferin Street, Toronto, Ontario, Canada M6B 3T5 416-781-9131
1155 Yonge Street, Toronto, Ontario, Canada M4T 1W2 416-934-3440

¡También somos su fuente para libros, videos y música en español!

Pauline
BOOKS & MEDIA

6209
$ 1.95

$1.95

ISBN 0-8198-5859-5

9 780819 858597

$0.99
348058
s6-
077-G
No Exchange
Media
Books

savers